MAKING CHOICES

WITH THE OUTER PLANET TRANSITS:

URANUS
NEPTUNE
& PLUTO

Mary Fortier Shea

M.A. Counseling Psychology

Please enjoy the information contained within. Learn from it and grow in your understanding of astrology, psychology, and spirituality. I have benefitted greatly from these insights, and I hope you do too.

Cover designed by Mary Fortier Shea

ISBN 978-1-930310-28-5

Printed in the United States of America

Published by Twin Stars Unlimited

Mary Fortier Shea

PO Box 301, Clinton, CT 06413

860-554-5031

maryshea@maryshea.com

www.maryshea.com

MAKING CHOICES

WITH THE OUTER PLANET TRANSITS:

URANUS

NEPTUNE

& PLUTO

Mary Fortier Shea

M.A. Counseling Psychology

Table of Contents

Table of Contents (cont.)

Table of Contents (cont.)

MAKING CHOICES

WITH THE OUTER PLANET TRANSITS:

URANUS

NEPTUNE

& PLUTO

Making Choices with the Outer Planet Transits: Uranus, Neptune, and Pluto

Introduction

Transiting outer planets, Uranus, Neptune, and Pluto represent three very different processes for change, growth and the breakdown of established structures. These three heavenly bodies are trans-Saturnian planets and this is important to remember. For a long time, astronomers and astrologers thought Saturn was the outermost planet in our solar system. It was considered the limit, the symbol of the end of our immediate awareness. Saturn is the last planet we can see unaided with our own eyes. But with the invention of the telescope, the discovery of Uranus, Neptune and Pluto followed. We broke outside the limits, physically, mentally, psychologically, and also spiritually. Together and individually, each in its own way, these planets are associated with breaking barriers.

Saturn rules structures that have stood the test of time and laws that were developed to rule the masses. It is the planet associated with setting limits that condense energy into matter. Uranus rules modernizations. It breaks the barrier by calling for improvements on what has been built and established. Uranus also signals a desire for freedom from all restrictions. It is the only planet which spins on its side while in orbit. For this reason, Uranus is associated with the rebel, the person who does not conform. Laws might be all right for the masses, but what about the individual test case. Those with Uranian freedom impulses want to understand how a broad-based law applies to their particular situation. They want to be the exception to the rule. In this way, Uranian methods chip away at Saturnian structures.

The principles associated with Neptune go beyond Saturn by testing for the spirit of the law. The question becomes, "what is the intent of this rule?" The law is only a reflection of the original purpose behind it. It is the Neptunian design to penetrate to the deepest meaning. Increased sensitivity is the mode by which this is done. Those who are sensitive to the spirit of the law, do not need the law at all. They innately do what is best by adapting the spiritual purpose to the specific situation. In this way Neptune indicates timeless principles that go beyond outdated Saturnian rules and rigid structures.

Pluto represents the next step in human development, i.e., empowerment. Pluto symbolizes the force needed to empower the lifestyle envisioned during the search for individual freedom and spiritual intent. Saturn at its worst can be the "herd mentality" with everyone thinking the same. Uranus is the ability to break away from the standard to think for yourself. Neptune indicates comprehension of Universal principles brought about by increased sensitivity. Pluto, the planet of power represents the strength to live the new system you create in your mind. Without Uranus, one can get bogged down in the norm. Without Neptune, one becomes a rebel without a cause. But without Pluto, one becomes a spiritual wimp, knowing and understanding certain beliefs, but unable to act on them.

Uranus, Neptune, and Pluto

Sensitivity to the outer planet transits

Every person is different in their sensitivity to the outer planets. You might be very sensitive to Pluto and not notice the passing of Uranus and Neptune. The best way to discern your sensitivity and response pattern is to look at the natal chart itself. For example, if you have a prominent and strongly aspected Uranus in your chart, you will probably experience strong change as a mode for growth. If Neptune is strong in your chart, you should be very sensitive to change on a more subtle level. You may not need external change in your life to be aware of a shift in consciousness. If Pluto is strong in your chart, you are more likely to respond to intense situations with power. Individuals are very different in their awareness of the processes associated with these planets. By watching your pattern of response, you can discern which planets are most meaningful to you. Go back over important events and turning points in your life to see which transits were occurring at those times.

Timing

The transits of the three outer planets can last for a couple of years, especially when a "triple transit" occurs. In this situation, the transiting planet passes in aspect to the natal planet three times; first going direct, then after turning retrograde, and finally as it moves ahead direct for the last time. A very few will experience five passes if the planet literally turns retrograde on the natal planet being transited. This process may take as long as three years for Pluto. The outer planet can have an effect on you for that entire period of time. Because we differ in our sensitivity to the outer planets, we cannot talk about a definite orb. It is different for different people. The process usually begins slowly, getting stronger as the transiting planet draws near and then fades out after it passes. Almost everyone will notice changes occurring when a planet is in orb by less than one degree, but with Pluto the process can start as much as five degrees out. Work with your transits proactively rather than waiting for them to happen to you. If you can, create an avenue of expression by planning an appropriate, positive experience during contact. For example, one man planned his first Kundalini Yoga class around his Pluto transit. That night he had his first out of body experience. A conscious choice such as this helps to focus and release your personal energy in a controlled way.

Uranus transits

Uranus indicates the need for change. Either major transitions or incessant fluctuations emerge as the pattern of manifestation depending on how the individual copes with his or her push for freedom. Transformations may occur quickly and require a long period of adjustment, or progress slowly, possibly occurring late in the transit and only after a long period of anticipation or restlessness. As a rule, most changes are expected, predicted, and initiated by the native him or herself. Many are carefully planned and well-executed, involving a minimum of tension and anxiety.

With Uranus transits, you cannot stay with the old structures. You must modernize and create more freedom in your life. By studying the transiting house placement of Uranus, the house placement of the natal planet transited, and the transiting aspect, you can see where changes are more urgently needed and more likely to occur. Conditions associated with the house position of transiting Uranus are likely to evolve significantly over the year and the focus of change will be directly related to the planet being aspected.

Increasing restlessness is the early psychological warning signal for this transit. The desire for change will increase as situations are outgrown. You will feel unsettled. If you wish to work with the process, welcome the opportunity for adjustment, and make all the necessary preparations. Start by asking questions. Consider alternative ways of handling issues facing you. Do not lock yourself into one pattern of growth. Allow changes and insights to develop naturally during the transit.

Generally, it is only when the individual thwarts needed changes, or tightly controls situations, that tensions manifest in the form of anxiety. These actions and emotions result from ambivalent feelings in those who resist their own process. These people get caught between a fear of change and a strong desire for the very change they fear. A dual mind-set takes over, one built on an approach to, and also an avoidance of, change. When one is unable to affect needed changes, the mind splits between two mutually exclusive goals and anxiety results. Eventually, the mental ambivalence and erratic commitments to two very different paths are reflected in fluctuating external conditions. Long overdue, yet still avoided changes, manifest in the environment as disruption caused by others, or by areas of neglect. Adding to the anxiety is a perceived loss of control over external situations. Eventually, the restlessness and tension rise to a feverish pitch until one finally agrees to make changes, or can no longer prevent their occurrence. When conditions reach this intensity, individuals usually make reactionary changes without careful consideration or adequate preparation. They do not have the tools to handle a process they have been avoiding all along. Sudden upheavals occur rather than welcomed transitions. If you would truly be in control of your own destiny, you would listen to the need for change and respond appropriately to the earliest hints of restlessness. You would give yourself the freedom to work towards a conscious transition before a crisis arose.

Consistent with the desire for change is the need for freedom. You cannot maneuver if you are locked in a restrictive environment. The push for freedom is a common precursor to change, but other times, the change itself is the motivating force behind the process. Sometimes, both mechanisms are operating and intertwined. Freedom allows the process of change to develop smoothly. Freedom is also a frequent by-product of changes once they occur.

Making Choices with the Outer Planets Transits

When you are functioning at your best and working positively with Uranian concepts, you move easily through a series of questions and alternatives, eventually making choices and taking independent action. You learn and grow from all encounters. Your desire for options, answers to questions, and alternatives to problems leads you to many different situations, persons, or concepts. It is important to watch what experiences you are drawn to during this time. Observation is a necessary step before choice. Do not resist the insights that follow. Take in fresh information. Learn to value all experiences. You will see that no one person, place or idea is perfect. The same is true of your existing circumstances to which you hold so tightly. This realization brings you to the door of choice, aware of changes that need to be made with possible options for the future.

The arrival of insight signals the beginning of the period of decision. You start by reassessing your involvements and commitments, and then choose to detach either internally or externally from those situations, persons, or concepts which restrict your growth, or no longer have anything to offer you. You learn as much from defining what you don't like as you do from defining what you do like. The changing environment, comparisons, and contrasts accentuate what is important and what is not. Take corrective action and adjust circumstances to your needs. Separations might occur, but not always. Detachment is a more accurate word, and you can detach internally while maintaining the external experience. But freedom and choice must arise on either the inner or outer plane. You must choose, otherwise the choices will be made for you.

Remember that this process of questioning, deciding, and independent action is an ongoing one occurring on many different levels simultaneously. Events might be sudden and complete, or reoccur in numerous small steps.

Uranus, Neptune, and Pluto

All transiting planets represent a creative process. Uranus is the creative process experienced through change. The exposure to various ideas, situations, and people stimulates original thought and sudden insight. One becomes accustomed to looking at life from different perspectives. The multifaceted approach encourages working with new ideas. In this way, the individual begins to participate in the process of change by creating his or her own options.

Uranus transits to the Sun

Uranus aspecting the Sun suggests a time when egotistical forces of the conscious personality must be released or transformed either internally or externally for growth to continue. This transit is like spring cleaning for the ego. Even though you pick up your house daily and keep it clean, sooner or later you must do spring cleaning. The windows need washing, the rugs need beating, and the walls need scrubbing. You clean the closets and throw out what is no longer useful while reorganizing what you wish to retain. The same is true of the ego. Eventually, you outgrow your present "beingness" and find that certain behaviors are no longer useful. This excess baggage needs to be eliminated or transformed. Uranus transits to the Sun indicate a time when this is most likely to happen.

It is natural to latch on to what works and stay with it. Familiarity breeds security, even when what is familiar is also burdensome. We all get "snagged" by a particular idea, fear, or mode of being. We put blinders on and refuse to see the major or minor changes that need to be made. We are afraid to let go of our positions, unaware of options. We fail to see beyond the needs of a snagged ego, desperate to maintain a passé position, fearful of what the future might bring, frozen in time and space.

Uranus is the planet which symbolizes freedom, desired or not, from a stalled position. The more resistant you have been in the past and the longer the forces of tension have been allowed to build up, the more powerful and less controllable the release. The more options you have available, the more likely you are to channel the changes in a productive manner. Certainly, the search for alternatives is crucial to assuaging fears, releasing tension, and directing results. You can move on to something better during this transit, or you can simply move on, willingly or not.

During the time of the Uranus transit to your Sun, significant life changes will occur, either externally or internally. Possible events include pregnancy and birth, career change or job transfer, marriage or divorce, relocation, or illness for you or someone close to you. Internal psychological transformations are just as likely to occur, even more so for those who have created the options. Included in the inner process are shifts from boredom to originality. Freedom replaces restriction. The final outcome, whether external or internal is associated with the amount of pent-up personal energy to be released and the range of options created. Resistance tends to lead to externalization and major events. If you are in touch with your masculine side, the process is more likely to be self-directed and generated by you. However, if you are not in touch with your masculine side, and especially if you are a woman who resists her more assertive urges, the period of growth is most apt to be focused externally on a significant man in your life.

Jean was a middle-aged woman having difficulties in her relationship to her husband. With her 12th house Sun, she wanted her husband to take the lead in most matters, but he refused. He rarely took the initiative and resisted most changes. Jean, on the other hand, had many ideas about what could or should be done, especially in regards to the home. She was the motivating force behind the decision to put an addition on their small home. The construction and renovation took over a year. During this time, Jean consulted with her husband on everything, but he offered more resistance and negativity than input. Jean wanted companionship in the building process, something her husband didn't offer. He objected to everything, making the process much more arduous. They fought repeatedly. Jean hated working alone and having to make decisions. She also hated having to push to get the smallest thing done. Jean was in a dilemma and stalled.

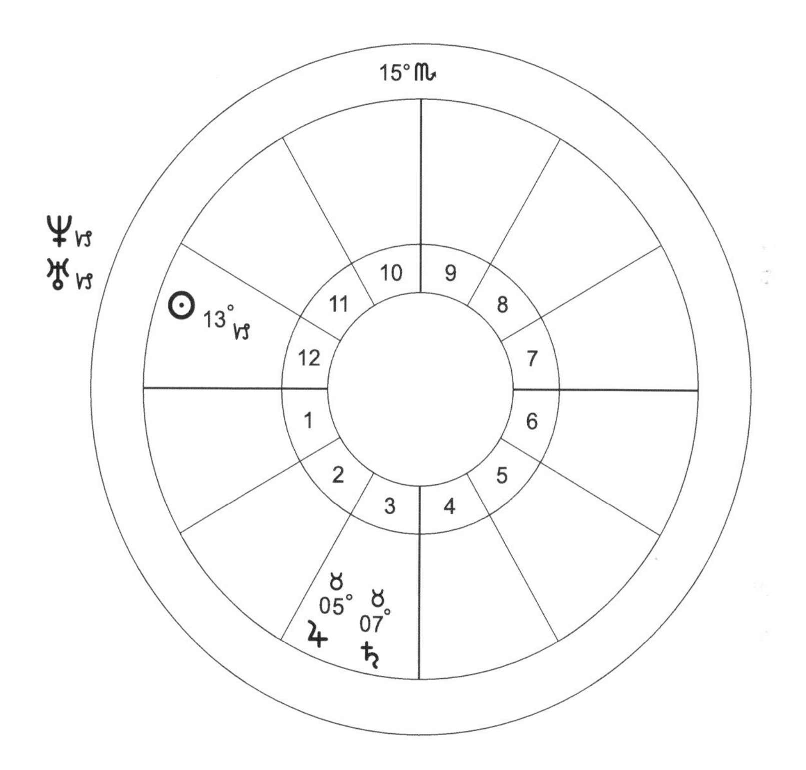

The push-pull situation went on until Uranus contacted Jean's Sun. At that point her husband became seriously ill and could offer no assistance or resistance whatsoever on any decision, even those associated with his care. Jean was forced to take complete responsibility for all decisions. With Neptune also transiting her

Sun, compassion rose. She saw her husband for what he was and understood what he could not be. She stepped back from trying to change him and assumed the very power she had avoided. She stopped asking for permission and he stopped giving her resistance. Because of his illness, she accepted the freedom she avoided to make decisions entirely on her own.

Uranus transits to the Moon

Probably the most common external manifestation associated with Uranus transits to the Moon is a change in domestic situation. Either you move from one place to another, or someone moves in or out of your home. A "musical chairs" routine can occur in the home as occupants move from one bedroom to another, or you change the house around to suit personal needs or preferences. Renovations, additions, repairs, and redecoration may be included in the grand plan for change.

A disruption in the home or family can lead to an emotional reorientation. On the other hand, emotional changes can be the motivating force behind modifications to the home. It's a question of which comes first, the chicken or the egg. Changes occur on more than one level. Emotional transformations go hand in hand with events occurring on the physical plane. While Uranus transits to the Sun indicate house cleaning for the ego, Uranus transits to the Moon indicate house cleaning for the emotions. Nonproductive patterns of response need to be eliminated from your repertoire so true intimacy can occur. Feelings of rejection, guilt, fear, and anger snag your development and lock you into stalemated conditions. Uranus transits to the Moon indicate a time when you can break away from patterns holding you back. The process of emotional release might be easier for women than men. A male who is not in touch with his emotions will tend to have a difficult time with a woman or mother during this transit. A significant female might be more in tune with tensions occurring in their relationship and initiate necessary changes. Females who are equally out of touch as their male counterparts will tend to have trouble with relationships, other females, or their mother. Though the purpose is always internal growth, the external triggering events can be different.

Relationships are bound to be affected by all this internal and external coming and going. You could become involved in a new relationship, or an old one might go through a period of transition or separation. Strong attractions are also possible at this time. If you feel caught in an emotional rut, dramatic changes are more likely to occur.

As your situation and emotional needs change, you face new issues and problems. Changing scenarios accentuate your ability or inability to handle emotions and relationships effectively. Negatively, emotional control is difficult and feelings are erratic. You are overwhelmed one day, detached and cool the next. You say or do things without considering the emotional consequences. But then, off-the-cuff reactions might be necessary to give you the freedom needed to make internal or external changes.

Positively, this can be a time of emotional potential, full of new feelings and greater intimacy. You could circumvent negative or debilitating emotions by creating new emotional patterns.

Karen became a new mother as Uranus transited her Moon. She had waited a long time for this. She was in her thirties when she married and wanted to start a family immediately, which she did. The role suited her well. Although it was a major change for her, she thrived with the new responsibility. In the early months, days were very hectic, but after things quieted down, Karen grew restless. Her husband was frequently away on business. His new company was doing well, but required much of his time. Karen missed seeing him, but knew not to dwell on negative feelings. She was used to working full-time, so she decided she needed a project to occupy her

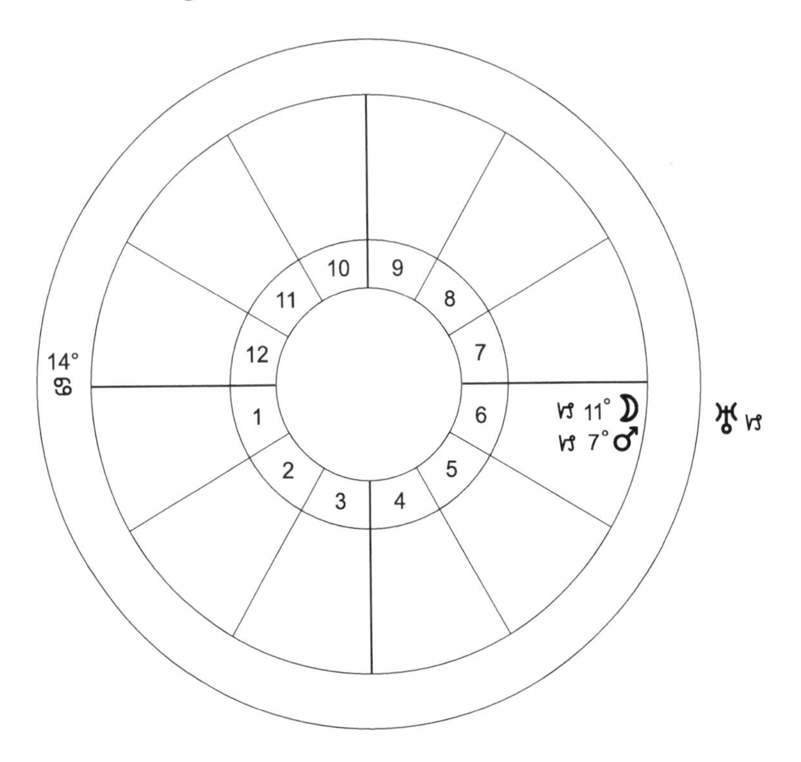

days. Since money was not a problem, she began to design a new home for her family. She drew up the plans with an architect, hired a construction crew, and oversaw the building process. The house went through many changes while under construction and is still not finished, but it has given Karen an outlet for her restlessness. Meanwhile she is still encouraging her husband to spend more time at home. She wants him to enjoy their good fortune.

Uranus transits to Mercury

Uranus transits to Mercury suggest a time when you are open to new and different ideas, methods, and ways of thinking. Insights arise from what you are learning and studying, or from concepts you develop on your own. Your thoughts grow more complex and profound as you learn to see things differently, viewing situations from many points of reference. Thinking becomes holographic with multifaceted connections into other areas of life, and many levels of interpretation. Straight-line thinking becomes passé.

A mental shift occurs from left brain critical processes to right brain creativity and understanding. Some find this shift difficult to make, but most make it easily. As facts become interconnected, the ability to learn, understand, and remember increases. Sudden realizations are the order of the day, and psychic openings are possible as intuition is heightened. Creativity grows and you are wise to take advantage of these impulses. Strive for originality by investigating new ideas and brainstorming with others. Open to new possibilities by eliminating left-brain resistances and favoring insight over rational thinking.

Implied with this transit is an increase in problem-solving ability. You are able to approach problems from a variety of perspectives and need not get locked into one way of thinking or being. Alternatives help you to break stalemates and negative thought patterns that hinder growth. You become mentally versatile, adapting to situations as they arise, or modifying circumstances to suit your needs.

The freedom to investigate many ideas occasionally leads to a very unfocused mind. Concentration becomes difficult if you constantly run from one project or concept to another. Thinking is interrupted by erratic impulses and insights. It becomes difficult for you to stay with one thought. New information is more exciting than reorganizing what you already know or concentrating on what you have to learn. If you must work on a lengthy project requiring a sustained mental effort, take frequent breaks and rotate tasks. Keep your interest level high by being very creative and spontaneous in your approach.

Making Choices with the Outer Planets Transits

Some individuals experience psychological strain during this time. Increased nervousness can usually be traced back directly to a stressful situation. Investigate the sources of tension. If possible, withdraw from situations which tax your mental and physical health. Practice relaxation techniques and avoid stimulants. Work on calming and nurturing your nervous system.

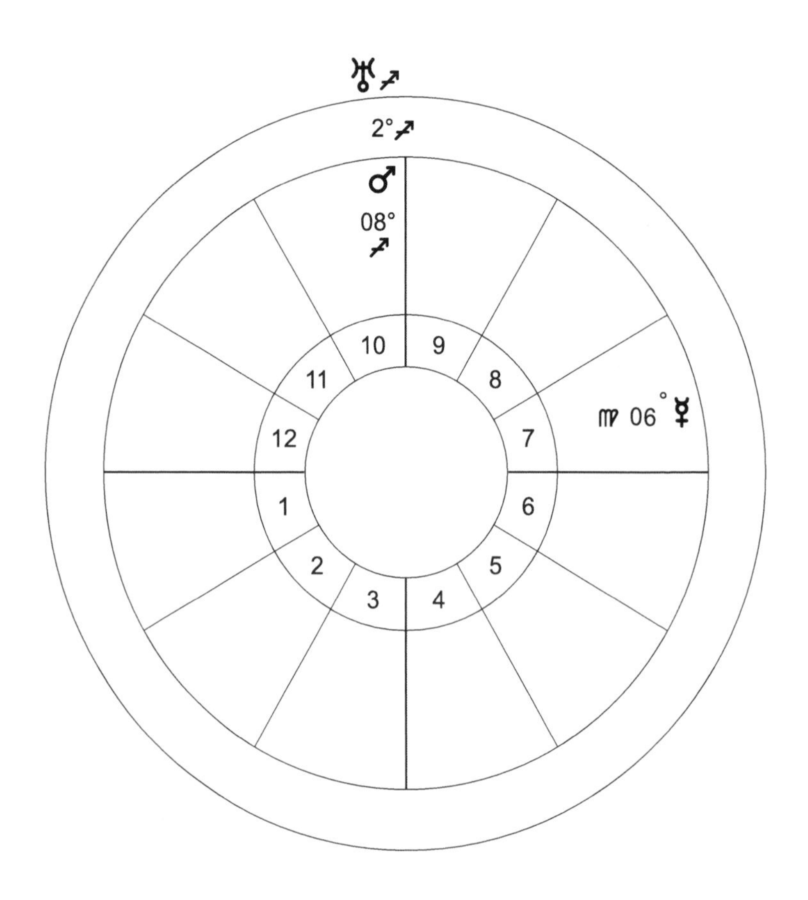

Debra took a job as an executive secretary for the head of a large company just as Uranus squared her Mercury. Soon after she started working, she learned that her job would involve some travel. At the time, Debra had a tremendous fear of flying and was incapable of getting on a plane. She would have panic attacks just thinking about it. She had to overcome her fear or she would lose her job. It was time to free herself from this debilitating phobia.

Debra decided to see if hypnosis would help her. During her weekly visits with the hypnotherapist, she learned to relax her body and reprogram her mind. She also learned about dream analysis and past-life regression. Things started to make sense as she began to work with her fear. Her intuition grew and she had great insights into her own healing. After a year, she was ready for the big test and flew across country for the first time. She is now a regular, (though admittedly sometimes reluctant), air traveler.

Uranus transits to Venus

Uranus transits to Venus usually denote changes in relationships. For some people, this will mean a sudden attraction and the excitement of a new love. Involvements can be very strong and very quick, but may not have staying power. It's easy come, easy go, and extremely exciting in between. Intense attractions might lead to marriage, but short-term affairs or loose associations are more likely. Turnarounds occur as friends become lovers, and some love relationships seem more friendly than intimate. Less conventional arrangements are also possible. These include clandestine or extramarital affairs, homosexual involvements, May-December romances, and long-distance love.

An already existing relationship can go through a period of adjustment. Difficult associations will most likely end or become on-again, off-again erratic involvements. Permanent or temporary separations are likely, especially when commitments are lacking or never kept.

But for those in healthy associations, changes will occur within relationships themselves. The Uranus transit will not indicate a break in ties or a loss of dedication between lovers. Bonds can instead strengthen. Changes will be discussed and agreed upon by both parties. One person might need the freedom to pursue a personal, career, or educational goal. A partner might be totally supportive of this move. Changes that affect both parties are likely, and issues of fidelity and open marriage are sometimes topics for discussion. External factors such as pregnancy and health also lead to change.

A general mood of disruption and restlessness permeates all partnerships, whether old or new. Expectations and behavioral patterns which were once taken for granted may now be nonexistent. New patterns emerge, and you can expect the unexpected. While the necessary adjustments are being made, the continuing disruption can cause conflict and temporary distancing between the people involved.

Financial changes will also occur when Uranus transits Venus. There may be a break or fluctuation in income because of commissions, incentives, layoffs, or part-time hours. Financial windfalls in the form of gifts and inheritances occur, but shortages and large expenses are just as likely. During this transit, some people become self-employed while others dispose of excess possessions.

Joan had been divorced from her husband John for five years. It was a very bitter divorce and the fighting had continued without stopping. Joan was always suing her ex-husband and he was always harassing her or counter-suing. Joan worried about money. She was dependent on John for support and had to pinch pennies to make ends meet. The support checks were generally late as John delayed every transaction. So, Joan went back to court to have her husband's salary garnished and the check deposited automatically.

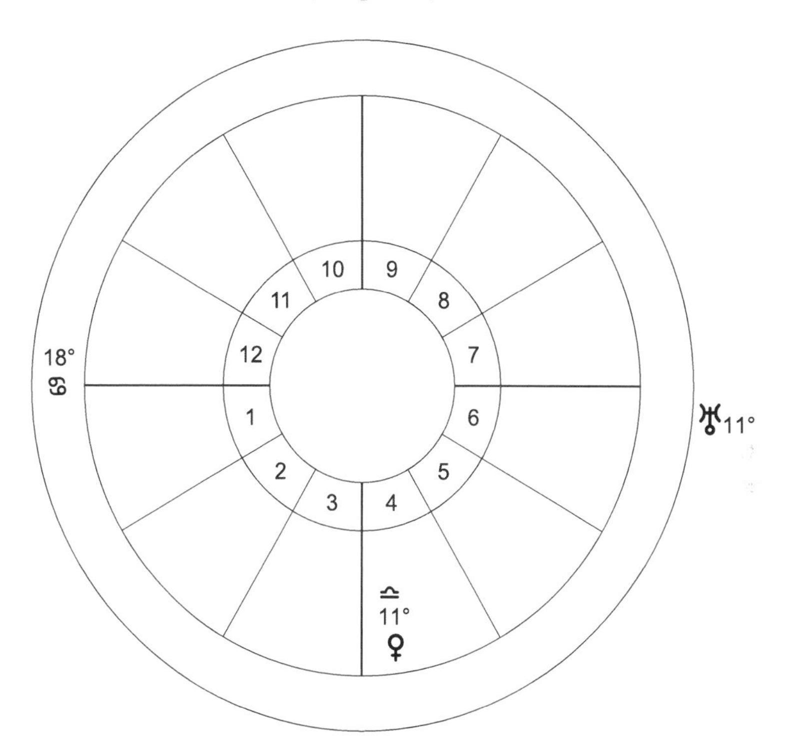

Things were quiet for a while, but then John retaliated. Using the account number for the automatic check deposit, he was able to withdraw all Joan's money leaving her penniless. He did this the day Uranus transited square Joan's Venus for the second time. Joan is now back in court suing her husband for return of the funds and also suing the bank for wrongful conduct and damages.

Uranus transits to Mars

Strong changes, usually self-initiated, are associated with Uranus transits to Mars. Freedom of action is the motivating force behind these changes and any restriction will be met with assertiveness, if not anger. You refuse to be trapped in a situation without options. You need room to maneuver. Anything boring is out. Anything new and exciting is accepted and encouraged. You reject tired routines and repetitive conflicts.

Changes range from a constant stream of minor adjustments to dramatic and sweeping transformations. Either form can be beneficial or detrimental depending on individual differences and the manifestation. Delays are unlikely since speed is of the essence. Once the process has begun, matters tend to move forward quickly. During this time, you may become more assertive or more detached. You may set concrete goals for the future or retreat from an unrewarding path. The tendency is to abandon situations that are no longer productive or comfortable. The amount of control you have over these changes depends on the choices you make or refuse to make.

Changes in relationships are common with this transit and are most apt to occur in those associations which involve sexual activity, or require an assertive or aggressive demeanor. New and powerful attractions are possible since sexual energy is heightened in those who are sexually experienced, or awakened in those who are not. Sexual experimentation increases as you investigate different forms of stimulation and diverse techniques. Occasionally, preferences change, as one is more likely to meet people with a different sexual orientation.

During this transit, behavior patterns might be somewhat erratic, and on-again, off-again situations will exist. Partners come together, relationships break up, and change is the order of the day. A need for greater freedom is usually the cause.

Ted was in his early thirties and very unhappy with his situation at home as Uranus transited opposition his Mars. His marriage was not stable. Although he loved his wife and they were still good friends, they realized that they were not happy together as husband

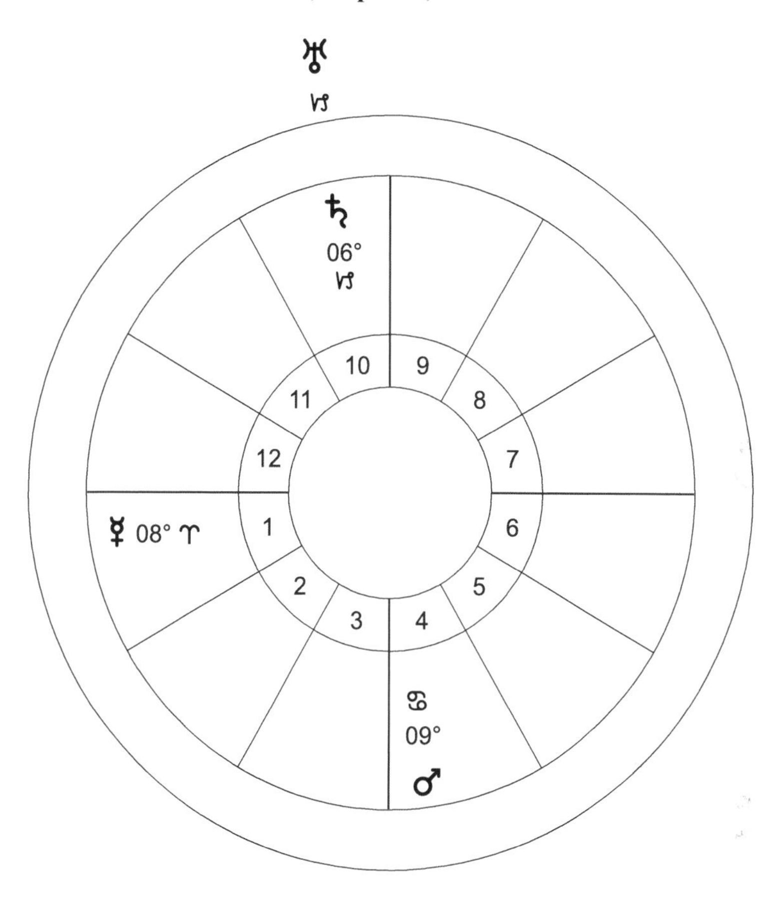

and wife. They had numerous fights which left Ted feeling drained and withdrawn.

Ted was also dissatisfied with his job. He had worked for a wonderful company for many years, but now, with the recession, the company was in financial trouble. His boss, who was normally pleasant to work for, succumbed to stress and took his anger out on anyone available. Job security was nonexistent. Ted felt trapped.

He did not have the education he needed to get ahead. Nor did he have the time to go to school, or a quiet place to study. Tension at home was high and his wife was constantly making demands of him.

Finally, Ted made some decisions and took action. He cut back on his hours at work, dropping to thirty hours a week. He refused to fight with his wife and moved out of the house and into an apartment, sharing expenses with a roommate. Their relationship got better as they both began to calm down. With his wife already working, they were able to budget their incomes and share the expenses of raising their daughter equally. This left Ted with enough money to pay for school and enough time to study. He is now continuing his education and dating his wife.

Neptune transits

Neptune has been interpreted as many things on many levels: confusion, deception, spirituality, and creativity (just to mention a few). But when Neptune transits a natal planet, there is a common theme that occurs over and over again, and is consistent with the psychological transition taking place. First and foremost, the Neptune transit is a call to understand and work with subtle and not so subtle human and Universal principles and energies. These forces are brought to your attention by an increased sensitivity on one or more levels. For example, during Neptune transits:

• You might develop allergies as your body becomes more sensitive to certain foods or environments. You learn to avoid those substances and situations which make you ill. Sometimes you have to work to identify the offenders.

• You may become more sensitive to those who are wounded, whether they are emotionally upset, spiritually in need, physically ill, or disabled. As sensitivity increases, compassion rises and you find a way to help. But if you are commonly taken advantage of and weakened by self-sacrifice, Neptune will herald in a time when you must eliminate activities which drain you.

• Your increased sensitivity may call you to creatively express yourself in new ways. This can be a time of great insight through symbol and metaphor.

• Spiritually you may be drawn to a religion, philosophy, or thoughts which have great import to your understanding of life and the world you live in. Unfortunately, what you understand and try to live may not be understood by others. If insights do not fit your present life situation, you can get caught between two worlds, not sure of the next step to take. Disillusionment can follow if your beliefs prove false.

• For some, the increased sensitivity, will become too much to bear. They will seek to withdraw from raw perceptions or drown their senses in drugs, booze, or addictions. Finding it difficult to accept, understand, and grow with their new sensitivity, they will feel compelled to retreat from it.

It is the increased sensitivity and the need to direct these sensations and subtle forces in a meaningful way which are the hallmarks of the Neptune transit. As the protective shell which keeps you immune to external influences sheds another layer, and your awareness grows a little more, you are offered a choice. You can either develop with, and learn from, these new sensations, moving to a higher understanding, or you can try to block out or ignore the new influences, staying with your old pattern of behavior. Sometimes the process is frustrating and arduous. You are often asked to give more when you have already given everything you have to a chain of events you do not fully understand. But there are rewards for those who stick with the progress and try to get an overview of the big picture.

Making Choices with the Outer Planets Transits

Choices are not limited to the spiritual plane alone, but can occur on the emotional, mental, and physical levels also. For example, Neptune on the spiritual level is associated with Universal Oneness, karmic laws, ideals, a strong trust in God, and higher beliefs which form the backbone of spirituality. The growth process on the spiritual level has ramifications on the other levels as well. Each level of experience supports and triggers the others. It is all the insights on all of the levels which eventually help you toward a more rewarding and fulfilling lifestyle.

The lower manifestation of a Neptune transit on the spiritual level is disillusionment with beliefs. The individual becomes entangled in despair, or fanatical concepts and outright fantasy. Distortions at the spiritual and philosophical level eventually cause distortions in perceptions on all levels of awareness as the trickle-down principle takes effect. Spiritual despair rather than enlightenment is the result. Hopelessness sets in and the support needed for growth is thwarted.

The same dichotomy of choices is present on the other planes also. At the emotional level, the individual is capable of great compassion and sensitivity towards others. This is a time when empathic understanding strengthens the bonds between loved ones. You are called to give more than you have in the past while expanding your circle of concern to those you might not know.

The more difficult manifestation of a Neptune transit on the emotional level is a susceptibility to anxiety and worry. The sensitivity which is meant to foster understanding instead heightens vulnerability to life, others, and the future. Fear prevails. There is no trust in God, Higher Self, or the Universal Plan emanating from the spiritual level to support decisions. One feels lost and abandoned, lacking both spiritual and emotional connections. In very negative situations, real relationships are not established and emotional deception and fantasy occur.

At the mental level, creativity and inspiration help to expand the individual's intellectual capacity. Neptune is more closely associated with right-brain activity than the left. New abilities and insights can develop in those willing to let go of preconceived notions and thought patterns. Observation, free-floating awareness, and an openness to seemingly irrational insights can lead to brilliant realizations.

Difficulties at the mental level involve confusion and deception. What you are told is different from what you intuitively feel. Changing beliefs and thought patterns leave you without a point of reference. You flounder because you are unable to make good decisions. New insights contradict old ways of thinking and you are unable to discern the truth. The development of right-brain processes breeds distrust. Creativity is thwarted, experimentation restricted. The child never gets to play. Without an understanding of the big picture, mental energy is wasted through a lack of cohesiveness. One focuses on insignificant details. There is no system, no rhyme, and no reason to thought, no purpose to the course you have set upon.

And finally, Neptune on the physical level is service to others. Principles filtered down from the spiritual, emotional, and mental levels begin to flow into daily practices on the mundane plane. There is a consistency; as above, so below. It is possible to physically manifest the spirituality you aspire to. You are able to do that which you believe, feel, and say. Neptune at its highest level of manifestation on the physical plane is a direct reflection of the enlightened promise made at the spiritual level.

When things start to go wrong on the other levels, it seems that only difficulties filter down to the physical level. When it rains, it pours! Confusion, disorganization and exhaustion are most apt to occur. You lack a total concept necessary to unify your actions and prioritize tasks according to their importance. You are overly sensitive on all levels without an understanding of how to handle that sensitivity or respond to outside pressures.

During Neptune transits, any of the above-mentioned insights or difficulties can occur. Sometimes actions are a confused mixture of ambivalent responses. This contributes to the confusion. The more focused the individual is on a search for answers and the need to understand the newfound sensitivity, the more cohesive actions will tend to become. A unifying principle at the spiritual level structures responses, focuses energy, and promotes understanding right on down the line.

Neptune transits to the Sun

Neptunian transits to the Sun indicate that the ego of the native is being challenged. Lessons in humility and vulnerability are common as egotistical responses to life are thwarted and denied. Personal identity is questioned, especially if you identify more with what you do than who you are. You cannot play a role during this transit; you must be real. Role playing leads to anger. Personality inconsistencies result in confusion. A personality crisis is likely for those who lose touch with self somewhere along the way. For these individuals, stripping away the ego and the personality facade results in an unstructured response to life and a temporary loss of control and direction.

During this time, you are more likely to be confronted with your own human frailties or those of someone close. Awareness of personal shortcomings opens you to understanding the shortcomings of others. Empathy becomes easier when you are no longer perfect yourself. We all suffer from a pandemic disease called humanness, and we all eventually die from it. But that does not mean we have to stop living now to accommodate someone else's character flaw. Martyrdom and victimization are an exaggeration of the issue if you give to the point of losing your sense of self. Your ego becomes so identified with a self-sacrifice role; you forget who you are. In these situations, personal or secondhand involvement with alcoholism, drugs, addictions, or a codependent situation is possible. Physical tiredness follows.

This transit is meant to arouse understanding and compassion. You are asked to give to those less fortunate and truly deserving. It is time to be less concerned with self-oriented interests and more concerned with the needs of others. But you cannot ignore the true self when setting standards for behavior. Wise giving is more intelligent and more beneficial than giving from guilt without purpose or understanding. Sensitivity leads to a stronger sense of self and an enlightened ego which chooses according to the needs of all those involved.

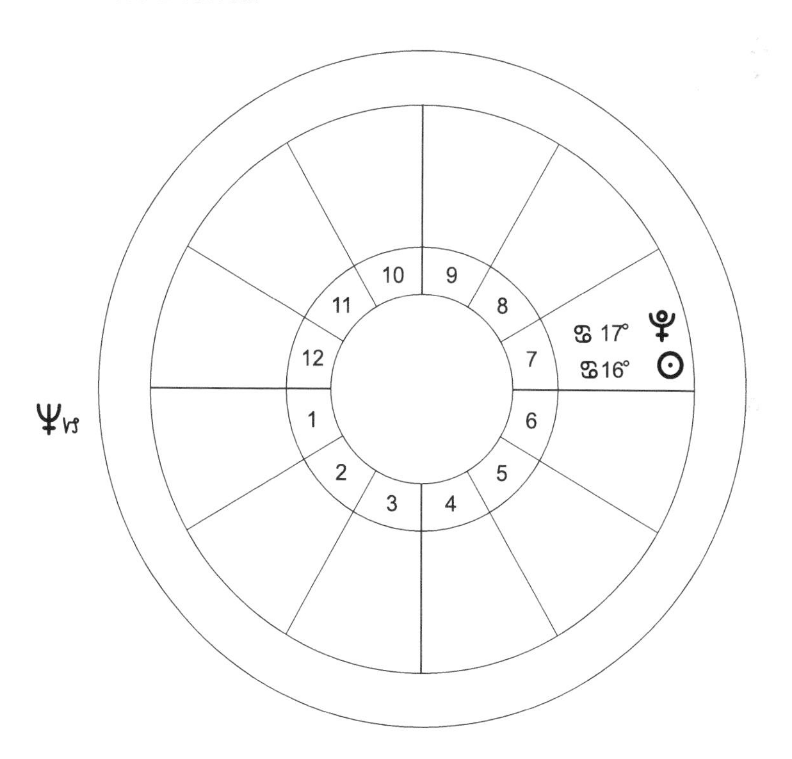

Making Choices with the Outer Planets Transits

Carol is a sixty-two-year-old woman who has been taking care of her mother all of her life. Her mother is now eighty-five years old and senile. She has been living with Carol and her husband for forty years. Carol feels overwhelmed by guilt whenever she entrusts the care of her mother to someone else. She will not hire a nurse to watch her mother, nor will she take her to a senior citizen daycare center. Placing her is a home is out of the question. Though her mother has periods of poor health, she could easily live another ten years. Carol feels physically drained and mentally trapped by her mother's need for round-the-clock care. She feels she has given up much of her own life to care for this woman who might now outlive her and/or her husband. Her husband is past the age of retirement, but has refused to stop working. They had always hoped to travel in their senior years, but with Carol's mother around this seems impossible and he does not wish to quit work and sit home all day with nothing to do.

As Neptune transits opposite Carol's Sun, she realizes that her ego has become so identified with the caretaker role that she has sacrificed her own needs and those of her husband. For years she has put off plans until her mother passed away. Now time seems to be running out while her mother's care becomes increasingly more demanding. Carol is being asked to "give wisely." Sacrificing out of guilt is draining away her energy. She has to look at the overall pattern of her responsibilities to make appropriate choices for herself and her family. She and her mother have had a codependent relationship for years. During this time, her mother had rejected the assistance of anyone other than Carol. Years went by and regrets won't bring them back, but with compassion and firmness, Carol can make changes that will balance the scales of giving and help her discover the part of herself ignored over the years.

Uranus, Neptune, and Pluto

Neptune transits to the Moon

Neptune transiting in aspect to the Moon indicates a time when intuition and compassion arise from a greater sensitivity to feelings not openly expressed or owned. While the ego and self-identity are challenged when Neptune transits the Sun, the emotional and intuitive nature of the native is the point of focus when Neptune transits the Moon. Emotional vulnerability increases as the unconscious, feminine, and receptive side of the individual is sensitized by subtle experiences that defy immediate identification and/or comprehension. Vague sensations and intuitive glimpses represent the initial intuitive or emotional input, and you don't know what you are picking up. What is this emotion? Are you sensing another's sadness? Is this vague perception an insight? Or is it all just your imagination?

Uncertainties leave you hanging as you await further information and developments. During this period, emotional situations cannot be controlled or structured, so you learn to accept what is offered. You also cope with emotional uncertainty, agreeing to relationships which are not clearly defined, giving without a guarantee of return. You view insecurity as a natural by-product of your situation and trust that things will eventually work out, one way or another.

Compassion and empathy are very much a part of the intuitive process and the movement towards acceptance. Here is a transit which really pulls at the heart strings because you identify so strongly with what others are experiencing. Sometimes this cognition clouds your perception of your own feelings. Emotional connections are made because you rise above judgmental attitudes and truly understand another's situation. You readily offer assistance and give more than you normally would. You let your nurturing nature flow and allow others to become dependent on you or you on them. You accept people as they are, weaknesses and all. During this time, you might care for someone who is ill or disabled, or you could simply care for another person more than you care for yourself and your own welfare. Neptune-Moon transits are a sign of self-sacrifice. It is common to see this transit in the charts of new parents and those with elderly relatives to nurse.

Spiritual or emotional idealism lifts your understanding to a new level. But putting someone on a pedestal leads to disillusionment and diminishes the possibility of genuine progress which could have been accomplished through recognizing and dealing with human weaknesses. Idealization is a blindness which creates unrealistic expectations and distorts perceptions while blocking out human faults. You deceive yourself when you avoid a truth more threatening than mystery. Situations remain clouded. Inconsistencies go unchallenged and deception is likely. When much is left unsaid, false assumptions take over. You fill in the gaps, seeing things not as they are, but as you hoped they would be. This continuing lack of accurate information is usually compounded by emotional estrangement. You become estranged from the person or truth you wish to avoid and your own emotional state. Anxiety and excessive worry grow. You miss the opportunity to use your intuitive insights in a constructive way.

Neptune transits to the Moon call us to recognize our emotional commonalities. We are all one and we can use our newfound sensitivities to foster understanding and emotional connections to others.

Peter is a middle-aged man who had been married for twenty-five years when Neptune transited square his Moon. He and his wife had drifted apart. Although they remained cordial with each other, they were no longer sexually or emotionally intimate. This left Peter in a state of limbo, neither married nor single. He did not know what to do about this, but avoided addressing the problem and acted as if nothing was wrong. This left his imagination free to

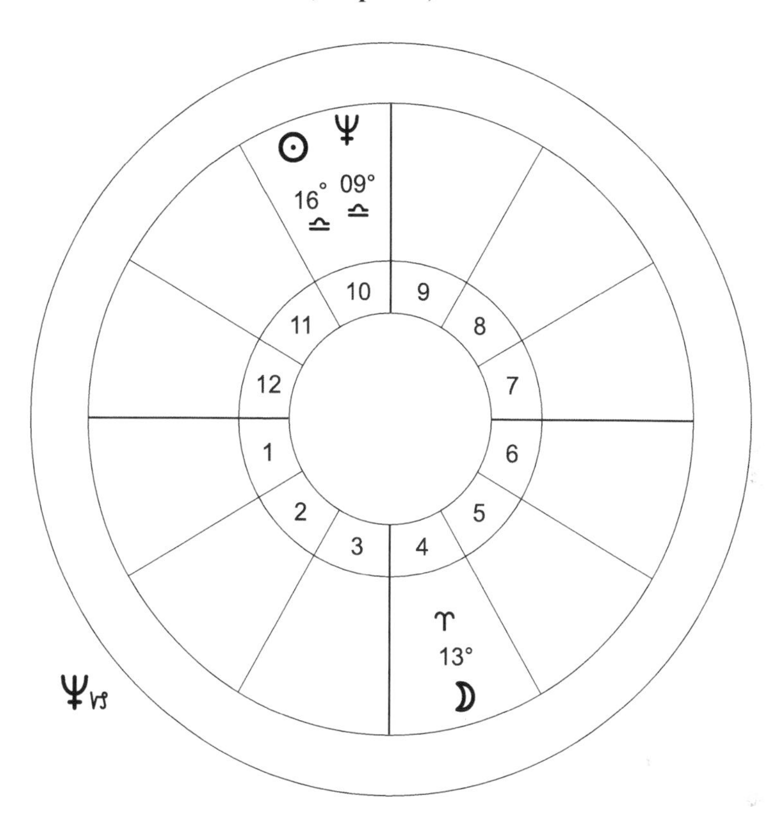

create rejection scenarios regarding his wife and attraction fantasies about other women.

Peter displayed a temper and was easily provoked, but never admitted his anger, only his annoyance. He frequently stated that he could not control his emotions. For years, his wife would compensate for his outbursts by "fixing" everything. But now, because of the estrangement, she was withdrawn and he was left alone to cope with his own moodiness, and to identify his own feelings. He found this process difficult.

During this time, Peter was forced to begin to comprehend his own emotional nature. He started to pay attention to how people reacted to his words and began to see why they withdrew. He learned to think before he responded and was able to gentle his words, especially to his daughter. Though still troubled by his homelife and still unsure of his relationship with his wife, as Neptune left his Moon and went on to square his Sun, he began to work with his situation in a more sensitive way.

Neptune transits to Mercury

Neptune transits to Mercury suggest development of the right-brain processes through studies of a spiritual, intuitive, or creative nature. It is a signal that a search has begun for subtle truth, possibly of a higher nature. Information of this type is not necessarily taught or given, but must be felt and experienced. Mental sensitivity increases as the native learns to work with those less clearly defined pathways to knowledge. Intuitive insights and psychic flashes are common during this transit.

Dealing with subtle truths can lead to some uncertainty and confusion in the thinking process. Increased intuitive or psychic awareness can precede the ability to weigh this information for its accuracy and symbolic content. It is sometimes difficult to discriminate between what is really an intuitive perception and what is more closely akin to worry, fear, or false hope. Symbolic dreams are sometimes mistaken for foreboding premonitions if a teacher is not available to guide the way. It is also hard to find practical applications for the increased sensory input. Idealistic concepts and insights can be unrealistic given your present situation. Mental stress and worry results from trying to integrate two different worlds (practical and spiritual), and two very different forms of knowledge (factual and intuitive).

Important facts or left-brain data that you receive may be partial, inaccurate, or vague. Some people will be the victim of intentional secrecy or deception. Without adequate information, you could be left hanging. Your normal points of reference for evaluating situations have changed. You easily become confused or misled, especially if you do not listen to intuitive perceptions and warnings. It may not be possible for you to accurately assess your circumstances and make an informed decision during this time. In older individuals, this transit might signal the beginning of senility. Medications can create a befuddled mental state regardless of your age. Neptune's most negative interpretation is a loss of mental capabilities through drug and alcohol use. This manifestation is more closely associated with an individual history of abuse, but problems can begin during this period. Those who normally turn to chemicals to help them cope with problems will find their rations escalating.

This transit is meant to foster great insight which leads to learning of a less obvious nature. Those who heed intuitive impressions, have the option of growing in their right-brain sensitivity and creative expression. (See the example chart for Neptune transiting Venus.)

Neptune transits to Venus

Neptune transits to Venus are associated with uncertainty surrounding financial situations and relationships. Changes occurring in these areas assist you in becoming more sensitive to inner qualities of beauty. You will be able to anticipate the shifting sands if you are conscious of subtle signals and messages.

Financially, this is a time when you can live without fiscal guarantees. You may have to if you are starting a new business or investing money in a new venture. Anxiety over money will not stop you and is likely to occur regardless of what you do or don't do. Those with a steady job will have paychecks affected by commissions, incentives, profit-sharing revenues, layoffs, or leaves of absence without pay. Salaries can also fluctuate because of part-time work, second jobs, or on-call hours. Under these conditions, you never know exactly what your salary will be until the check arrives. In rare situations, you could be unemployed and not know where your next dollar is coming from.

Changing circumstances, such as relocation, divorce, illness, large purchases, or major sales also affect the amount of money available to you. Many times, it is impossible to predict the effect these changes will have, especially when several variables are involved. If you expect money from others in the form of a loan, gift, or inheritance, you cannot be sure how much you will receive and when you will receive it. Regardless whether or not financial uncertainty is job related, monetary uncertainty exists in some form or another, but it need not be a serious problem. This is a good time to foster a strong appreciation of the nonmaterial side of life and allow your appreciation of the inner qualities to grow.

Neptune transiting Venus can indicate the growth of unconditional love. Significant emotional relationships become more supportive as partners become sensitive to each other. The subtleties of unspoken preferences are made known. You yield to your partner's needs, sometimes neglecting your own. Empathy and compassion increase as inner beauty is appreciated and allowed to blossom. External trappings are devalued and what you materially own and share is not as important as what you are willing to give emotionally.

If you are not already married, you or your partner may not wish to make a commitment at this time. New or less stable love relationships tend to lack definition and clarity. The situation may be such that you can't even label your relationship or give it a name. In any relationship, your partner's intentions may be unclear or actions contradictory. He or she may come and go, appear and disappear, say one thing and do another. One minute you know you are loved, and the next minute you are not so sure. It's difficult to know where you stand. While in this limbo, the relationship remains suspended in time, without a guaranteed future, or a present reality. Clandestine relationships are also common with this transit.

No relationship comes with guarantees to begin with, but with Neptune-Venus contacts the security can be even less evident. A persistent sense of confusion can cause you to misinterpret what is actually occurring. You don't always see the truth. This is most likely to happen when one or both partners are ambivalent or deceptive. At worst, there are lies to contend with. Because of the lack of clarity, idealization and deception might occur, making partners seem too good to be true. Aggrandizement of this sort can only lead to disappointment.

The best relationships breed compassion and sensitivity. Lovers who are honest and open with one another deepen their commitment and grow to appreciate each other's inner qualities.

Gloria was a divorced middle-aged woman who lived with a man named George for fifteen years. During much of this time, George had a series of second mistresses. As time went by, Gloria felt less and less loved and more and more insecure. But Gloria was afraid to leave George. She had never been on her own and she was afraid she could not make it financially. Although she earned a good salary, she was heavily in debt and lived rent-free with George.

Life continued like this until Neptune began to transit Gloria's Venus, Mercury, and Moon. She met Larry, a very wealthy man she grew to both love and loath. The two made plans for a business and life together. After only two months, Gloria left George, agreeing to marry Larry. They contracted to have two houses built, one for investment and one to live in. They made a bid on a restaurant. But even before the wedding, problems began to emerge as Larry's checks began to bounce. He was about to close on a seven-million-

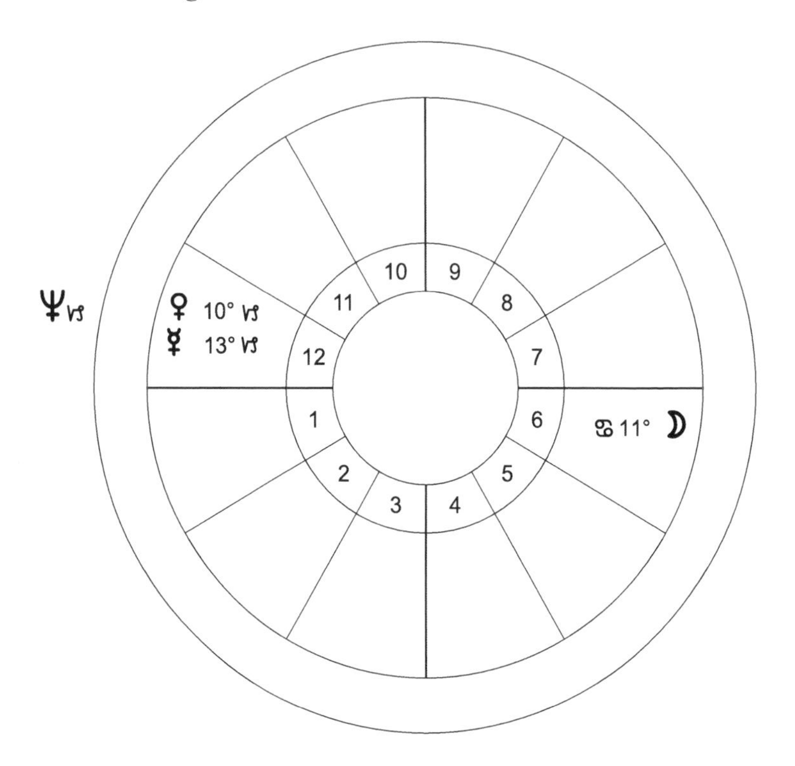

dollar deal and had cash flow problems. Gloria borrowed money and covered thousands of dollars' worth of checks.

Immediately after their August wedding, the check for the two houses bounced and Gloria began to suspect that her husband was not the millionaire he purported to be. She caught him in one lie after another. She confronted him with the evidence she had gathered and only then did he admit the deception. Gloria had enough sense to get out quickly. She immediately filed for an annulment.

She was evicted from her new home after only two months. Now she was without a place to live and was in worse financial shape than before. Unable to depend on anyone but herself, she started to take control and make some decisions. She rented an apartment in a building with security guards and friendly neighbors who watched out for each other. She went to garage sales and filled her apartment with beautiful furniture. She closed all the accounts she had with Larry and wrote all the creditors. She sued him for the money she lost.

Gloria is thankful that Larry got her to leave George, but she realizes that if she had been braver, she could have left on her own. She was used to George's deception, but she had not trusted her intuition when it came to Larry. There were many clues along the way and a deal "too good to be true."

Neptune transits to Mars

While Pluto transits to Mars imply actions that are unconsciously motivated, Neptune transits to Mars imply actions which have no obvious motivation at all. There is a great deal of uncertainty as to the direction you are headed in and the goal you intend to reach. You ad-lib life with no definitive need or desire directing your course of action. In some situations, careful planning is not feasible. Surprise events or unexplained twists of fate can occur, disrupting your schedule and leaving your previous course of action hanging and incomplete.

Uncertainty and confusion seem to go hand in hand with this combination and contradictory actions are possible. It is easy to stray from your original purpose when goals are not clearly defined. Some people might view your actions as confusing or inconsistent. It is easy for others to misinterpret what you are doing when your direction is unclear. This is a time when you can keep your plans secret, but if you are open to suggestion, objective feedback will help you remain well-grounded and consistent with your stated goals. Take time to listen to what others have to say.

If you do follow a specific plan of action, there are probably no guarantees that your actions will pay off. For example, if you are working on a research project that is a long shot, it's questionable whether or not you will see a practical return on your investment of time and effort. Employment might be unpredictable with rumors of layoffs, or changing company politics and office procedures. Despite bleak predictions, you might decide to trust things to work out and continue on the course you have set.

You have the ability to function despite uncertainty. Inner guidance is especially strong and projects can become almost effortless if you are sensitive to the universal flow of energy. You can be correct in assuming success even when the odds are stacked against you. But if you idealize your situation and miscalculate the results, you will be disillusioned when your efforts are for naught. Misguided endeavors are consistent with Neptune transits to Mars, especially with the more difficult or stressful aspects such as the square and the opposition. Therefore, you must consider carefully your intentions and actions. Be ready with an alternate plan if matters do not progress.

Humanitarian pursuits and volunteer efforts are also associated with Neptune transits to Mars. You willingly give your time and energy to a worthy endeavor and are able to sacrifice your own needs and desires.

The spiritual aspects of sexuality can awaken in you now. Perhaps it is time to be more careful with your body. Who you have sex with effects what you think of yourself and what you believe about others. New subtle physical and nonphysical energies can be felt by those most sensitive. You may wish to investigate Tantric or Tao sexual practices (eastern traditions) and become more versed in the exchange of energy taking place during love-making.

Jan was in her mid-thirties, working full-time and attending graduate school when she became pregnant unexpectedly. She had planned to continue her education, but now did not know what to do. She had recently remarried and her older husband did not wish to have any children. He had three from a previous marriage. They had just purchased a new home and the mortgage required two incomes. Jan's husband pressured her to have an abortion, and she was very torn. She did not want to threaten her new marriage, but she did not want to abort the child either. The decision went back and forth for weeks. It was during this time of turmoil that Jan

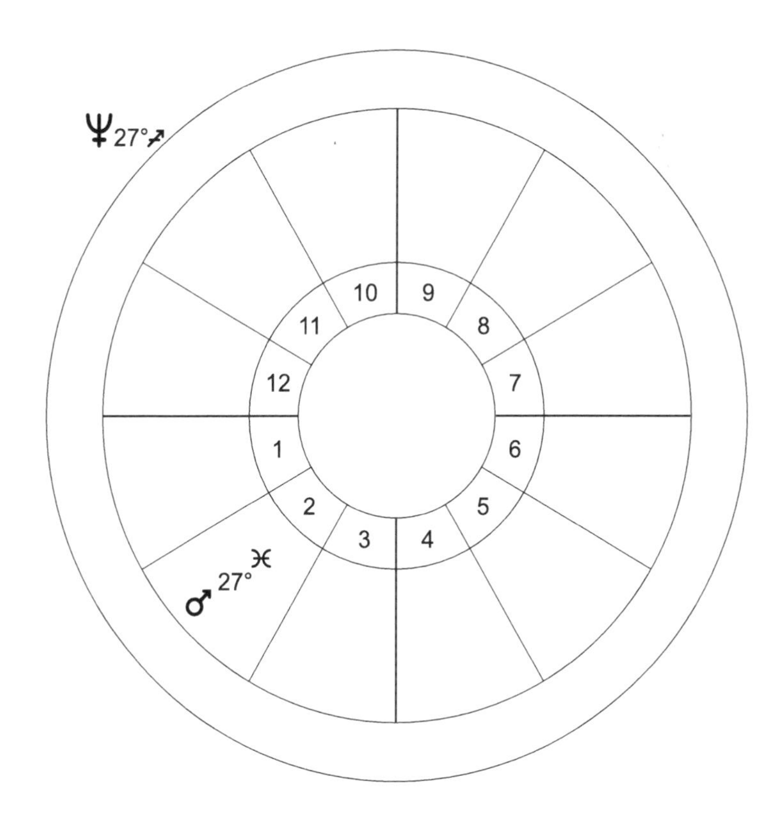

began to feel like the unborn child was a comfort to her. She sat talking to the baby, sang songs, and read it books. She felt a gentle mixing of energy within her body. This was her first pregnancy and it was a time of discovery. She decided to take the chance, school or no school, job or no job, husband or no husband. She rearranged her schedule so she would have time off when she needed it most. Reason might have indicated a different behavior, but Jan went with the subtle feelings she felt.

Pluto transits

When Pluto transits a planet in the natal horoscope, the balance of power begins to shift and you might gain or lose power during this time. You want to gain so that you will have the option of living your life according to the principles set down during Uranus and Neptune transits to your natal planets. Without empowerment, you will be forced to live by someone else's rules. You can strengthen your position naturally or use force. The growth-oriented response is to empower both yourself and others, internally and externally. There is much to be gained here by everyone from a kinetic human exchange.

Unfortunately, many find the empowerment task difficult to accomplish under the best of circumstances. Fears from the unconscious magnify threats to personal power causing defensive or offensive reactions. The perceived danger associated with a Pluto transit is the possibility of losing control over your own life. As combatants take a stance and stake out a claim, situations escalate and complications arise. Complex scenarios are the hallmark of the Pluto transit. Problems tend to be compounded by numerous subplots. There are no clear-cut answers to questions or perfect solutions to problems and one can easily become emotionally overwhelmed by their circumstances.

To gain power and move forward during a Pluto transit, you must understand the Path to Empowerment. This includes the extent and source of your personal power, how to best use or expand it, and where you are headed. Once these parameters are set you can move forward decisively by anticipating the next step toward growth and having the courage to take it. You cannot begin to do this until you understand where power needs to be applied. This is a crucial point to understanding the Pluto transit. The path splits here. There are only two broad choices, only two points of reference. Either you apply power internally, intent on maintaining and acquiring inner strength and knowledge, or you apply power externally, intent on fulfilling your personal or professional ambitions in the world arena. Although both orientations might be connected or follow one another in the final analysis, your reactions or goals during this transit and your effectiveness in the end are determined by your ability to discern the most powerful and appropriate action at any given time. The nature of the transit is that you must choose and choose wisely to progress. You cannot be wishy-washy. The longer you delay the decision, the more complex the situation becomes. Vacillation leads to complications and power leakage since definitive action does not take place and you undermine yourself. It is only when you come down firmly on one path or the other that your course of action becomes clear no matter how complicated the situation becomes. Under these circumstances you will progress steadily. Incorrect choices will be obvious since all actions in keeping with an inappropriate path will lead to failure and frustration.

The problem with the Pluto transit is that many people automatically assume a defensive or offensive position before they have considered using power in a positive and transformative manner. Fear speaks louder than insight with this transit and it is easy to lose your way and overreact. One engages the enemy without fully understanding the root nature of the threat or choosing an appropriate course of action.

Path of internal empowerment

What does it mean to choose internal empowerment? It means that who you are is more important than what you do, and what you understand is more important than what others think. It means you practice personal wholeness, a process by which individual integrity is maintained regardless of the external situation.

What do you gain from the process of internal empowerment? You gain freedom of personal action. Since all decisions are based on your personal value system, the possibility of interference is removed. You are not dependent on external criteria or results. It is not what you do, but who you are in the processing of doing or not doing that is important. You maintain a goal of trueness to self. Inner calmness sets in and you are able to focus and not lose momentum. There is an efficiency of thought and deed. Power is not split between two courses of action, but used in a consistent manner. Emotional overreactions are eliminated and therefore complications based on fear are kept to a minimum. You easily release counterproductive situations and personality traits. You control yourself internally and remain fearless. You influence others indirectly through the power of your calm presence and example. Issues are handled rationally by all parties. De-escalation occurs. Power is conserved.

Techniques for gaining and maintaining internal power

For internal empowerment to occur, growth and inner transformation must be emphasized over external results. Those who are sensitive to inner transitions understand the movement taking place regardless of external circumstances. You detach from what others think. You accept conditions as they are. This is the way of no resistance and there is minimal pain when it is followed. If two people fight over a rubber band, the one who lets go first doesn't get hurt. To truly practice the path of internal empowerment you must know when to let go and then do it with great regularity. The way of no resistance is the course of action to choose when there is nothing you can do which will make a difference in the long run. Matters are out of your hands. Any attempts at controlling outcomes will lead to frustration and lost power. This is also the course of action to take when you are in a very weakened state and have no more to give. You must focus inward to recover.

It is natural to want to fix things. But sometimes we try to fix things that are not our responsibility. It might be better not to take action and allow situations to develop on their own. This conserves energy and power.

Internal loss of power

For some, gaining power starts with preventing the loss of power. Certain character traits can erode personal strength. Reactionary blind spots get you in trouble. Psychological buttons bring forth an immediate response of a less than intellectual nature. As you get out of control, fears arise, tempers flare, and conflicts escalate. Weaknesses must be recognized and corrected before someone uses them to his or her own advantage against you.

You can also lose power by remaining in circumstances which are nonproductive and draining. These situations have no maintaining power of their own and are only preserved through the force and power of your own will or someone else's. I am speaking specifically of relationships and positions which are passé. Healthy circumstances will be sustained naturally and will not require extraordinary methods or effort.

Some people use psychological insights to control and block their own growth. They set up a negative pattern of stagnation wherein information is not accepted, but twisted to fit previously conceived notions about life and self. Insights become weapons against growth and understanding. Contradictory realizations are suppressed or misinterpreted by the ego. A fixed mind-set is imposed on all information. In a very negative situation such as this, the power associated with increased Plutonian awareness and its creative potential is never realized.

Misuse of the inner Plutonian process creates an inability to continue on the life path until issues are resolved and lessons are learned. Stagnation occurs when the individual is afraid to progress to the next level of comprehension and misinterprets all available information.

Path of external empowerment

What does it mean to choose external empowerment? It means to take action. If you have an idea that can make the world a better place, you implement it. The emphasis in not on what you think or know internally, but the application of knowledge to an external situation with a specific purpose in mind. Results are important and sometimes the ends justify the means. What you accomplish is more important than who you are. You establish a goal and go for it, holding to the highest good for all those involved. Personal power is used to make things happen and if it is done correctly, empowerment occurs.

What do you gain from the process of external empowerment? You gain results, confidence, and position. The environment changes because you directly influence others and situations. You gain freedom of action since you are the one in control. In the best of circumstances, many of the participating parties become stronger because of the empowerment process.

Techniques for gaining and maintaining external power

One way to gain external power while also conserving energy is to anticipate and circumvent problems before they occur. Energy follows thought. There is a natural progression to every chain of events. Those who are perceptive can anticipate the next move and stay one step ahead of the game by using de-escalation techniques to defuse explosive situations. Respond to anger with calmness and intelligent insight. Create alternatives and negotiate compromises which are win-win situations. Provide avenues for the release of tension before things get out of hand.

To gain the most empowerment from this path, kinetic interactions must occur. This leads to the creation of power for all those involved. Perhaps an example is the best way to clarify this process. The Dalai Lama, who is exiled from his own country, preaches and practices nonviolence in all things. Others have been drawn to his teachings and he has gained a following by bringing Tibetan Buddhism to the West. He is a Nobel Peace Prize winner and 1991 has been called "The Year of Tibet." Many people were empowered by his insights, but he also gained external empowerment from the kinetic interaction.

Anytime anyone establishes a goal which is clearly good for all those involved, it catches fire and is embraced. Kinetic interactions create power for all those involved. To walk this path, you must be as concerned with the welfare of others as you are with your own gratification. When others realize your good intentions, all fears abate and creative solutions arise. In daily living, seek out those situations of heightened power and kinetic interchange.

External loss of power

One reason for losing external power is a lack of concern for others. There is no respect for the highest good of anyone. You defend your territory only and do not care about the implications to others. Others perceive a threat to their position and barriers go up. Fears magnify and defensive and offensive attacks begin. Power struggles ensue. No one is totally right and no one is totally wrong. Everyone is caught in a cycle of reactionary responses that only complicate issues. Always be aware of the interactive process and the role you play in any battle. Blaming others for your problems distorts perceptions of self.

The other reason you lose power is a lack of concern for self. You undermine your own position or surrender power to others. A world without struggle is an ideal, and not reality. At some point in your life, it may be essential to take a stand. Certain injustices must be corrected for everyone to progress. Sometimes the only viable option is to fight back. Always be aware of the struggle you take on. Go for the simplest task that gets the job done. It is usually easier to correct a situation than to convince your opponent he or she is wrong. It is easier to get forgiveness after the fact than permission before. Seek the quickest solution. Do not get locked into unnecessary long-drawn-out struggles. Do it right and get the job done. Power struggles are expensive in terms of time and energy. Some are essential to growth, others are self-inflicted. Know the difference and don't waste your time on unnecessary or nonproductive conflicts.

The most efficient use of power exists on the internal plane. It is much easier to use energy to control your own reactions than to seek power externally. However, there are times when you must take action. In these instances, wield power wisely.

Pluto transits to the Sun

When Pluto transits the Sun, empowerment can occur either through awareness of self or struggle with others. The more attuned you are to your own personal power and any lacks your might have, the more likely you are to grow through awareness. Insights into power are heightened. You become acutely perceptive and easily observe how people get, maintain, use, and abuse power for personal gain or loss, and control of others. Power usage in everyday situations becomes more obvious, but even subtle shifts in power are evident as you learn to recognize psychological motivations and manipulations. It is only when you identify the manipulative tactics aimed at you personally that you begin to dismantle the controlling influences of others. This process by itself is very empowering.

Experiencing an upsurge in personal power or the lack thereof can also occur through conflict. You might have to defend yourself from an attack by a controlling or angry person. These situations are more likely to occur to victim personalities and those who do not know how to defend themselves. You do not have to be swayed by guilt, fear, or irrational accusations. Learn to neutralize these negative influences. Awareness of manipulative tactics is particularly helpful in deflecting blows and dealing with attacks on your character.

Some individuals study psychology during this transit. Others enter therapy or consciousness-raising groups. Psychological awareness breeds power. Regardless of the educational background, many people notice examples of obsessive, compulsive, phobic, neurotic, or manipulative behaviors in themselves or others. Unconscious needs are intensified. You see your own shadow reflected in the people you meet and situations you encounter. A cleansing of negative behavior patterns can take place in those who are introspective about their own actions.

Professional ambition is one of the more positive and noticeable manifestations of this transit. You are more likely to start you own business and become self-employed. The desire for power and self-control can reach into any area of life. Learning to deal effectively with power on many levels is the hallmark of the Plutonian transit.

Marilyn was married and had one teenaged son. She had been an agoraphobic for years. She would never leave the house and was afraid of open spaces. As Pluto began to make contact with Marilyn's Sun, she decided to seek therapy for her problem.

While in counseling, she realized how powerless she was. She had no financial security. Her husband had put them on the brink of financial disaster by gambling and spending money extravagantly. They were deeply in debt.

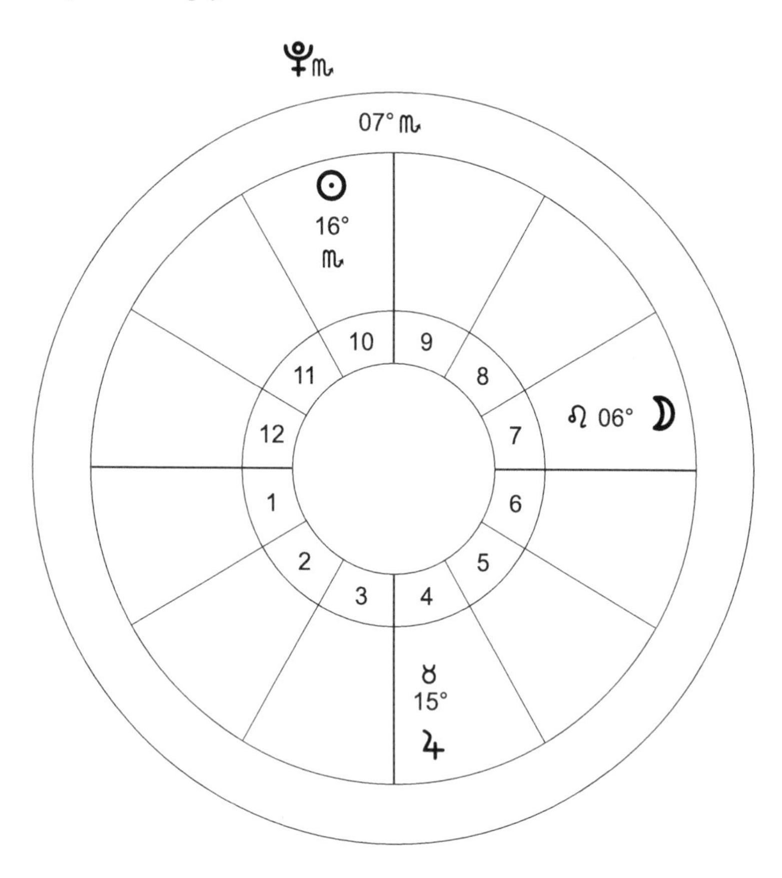

As the months passed, Marilyn went on outings with her therapy group and began to leave the house on her own. She grew stronger mentally and became more assertive in her relationship with her husband. When he was about to leave on a week-long golfing trip they couldn't afford, she confronted him with their unpaid bills and financial problems. She demanded to know what he intended to do about them. He patted her on the head and said, "You'll think of something." Then he left.

Marilyn did think of something and it only took her one week to do it. She decided she had progressed as far as she could internally. Thanks to her therapy group and therapist, she had made numerous inner changes, but now she needed to make some external changes to have power over her life. It took her two days to find a full-time job. She wrote all the credit card companies and disavowed any responsibility for her husband's bills. She established her own credit and separate bank accounts. Then she saw a lawyer, filed for a legal separation and had all the locks changed on the house. When her husband came home after one week, his clothes were packed and on the porch, along with a note that said, "I thought of something."

Marilyn had empowered herself internally as much as she could. When the time came to shift gears to the external process, she was able to do so. She chose to use her personal power swiftly and in the most efficient way.

Pluto transits to the Moon

When Pluto transits the Moon, the emotional makeup is complicated by unconscious influences. Emotions are tainted by events or complexes from the past, and you relive a former happening in an immediate and present situation. The garbage can of your own mind opens up so you can survey the contents and eliminate the trash. Feelings seem more volatile, intense, and even overwhelming. Reasoning becomes based on emotional factors and sometimes defies logic.

Relationships are likely to be affected and unconscious influences can distort communications. You or someone close might need counseling. If the other person is less than rational, you must deal with issues in an insightful way. This is a good time to become more aware of how psychological games affect you emotionally. You may merely observe these influences or you may be directly involved, playing either manipulator or manipulated. If you are feeling insecure, you might cling to others and try controlling them.

At their worse, Pluto transits to the Moon imply a major emotional power struggle. Though you may think you are struggling with another, you are also struggling with yourself. For example, suppose you have limited means, but are married to a wealthy person who is very tight with money. Since you resent this person's power over your economic situation, you withhold sexual relations. You have now gained some power over your spouse's life and the two of you have established a power struggle which complicates your relationship. Although you have succeeded in controlling your spouse's behavior to some extent, you have not gained any power over your own existence. Your situation has not improved much and you are still without financial recourse. There are more positive ways to handle this situation. Either one or both of you could decide to enter counseling to resolve this problem. Or you could get a job, earn your own money and frustrate your spouse's attempts to control you. Emotional blackmail and manipulation are consistent with this transit, but they only work if you allow another person to have control over some portion of your life. As soon as you begin to control yourself and take responsibility for your own well-being, manipulators lose all power.

Not all Pluto-Moon transits involve difficult circumstances. Writers, counselors, psychology students, poets, artists, and those whose work depends on their ability to understand human nature use this transit to gain insight. It is the awareness which is significant and not the struggle itself.

Knowledge brings power. Use this time to become aware of how unconscious drives affect your life. A very pleasant reason for being so emotional is an involvement in a new and exciting romantic relationship. Another possibility is the birth of a child. All relationships, even those which are established, are subject to transformation.

Domestic situations can also change. You can move, renovate, add on, or tear down. Roommates might come or go. The changes occurring in the physical home are symbolic of the internal emotional changes taking place. (See the example chart for Pluto transiting Mercury.)

Pluto transits to Mercury

Pluto transits to Mercury indicate a time when the conscious mind is more apt to be aware of unconscious material and psychological complexes. This awareness may originate from naturally occurring insights into human behavior or educational pursuits. You are better able to perceive what is unspoken or hidden. Mind games and motivations will be clear to you even when they are not verbally stated. Awareness is not all one-sided. You will be as aware of your own unconscious nature as you are of the complexes of others. Being aware of these psychological forces can be stressful, especially if you know more than you are capable of handling or the realizations come too quickly. In these cases, seek counseling.

You might be involved in a verbal battle over ideology, religion, or the truth. Others might doubt what you say, or push you to defend what you know or think on a given subject matter. The implication here is that knowledge is power and it is not taken for granted that you speak the truth. You must stick with your story to be heard. If you would convey wisdom and insight, you must make your words relevant and understandable to others.

A passion for learning is associated with this transit. Obsession with any topic is likely, but certainly an obsession with any occult practice is common. All forms of information are valuable whether they come from a book or the observation of life. Great insights can be gained from journaling and creative writing. This is a time meant for those who wish to know more.

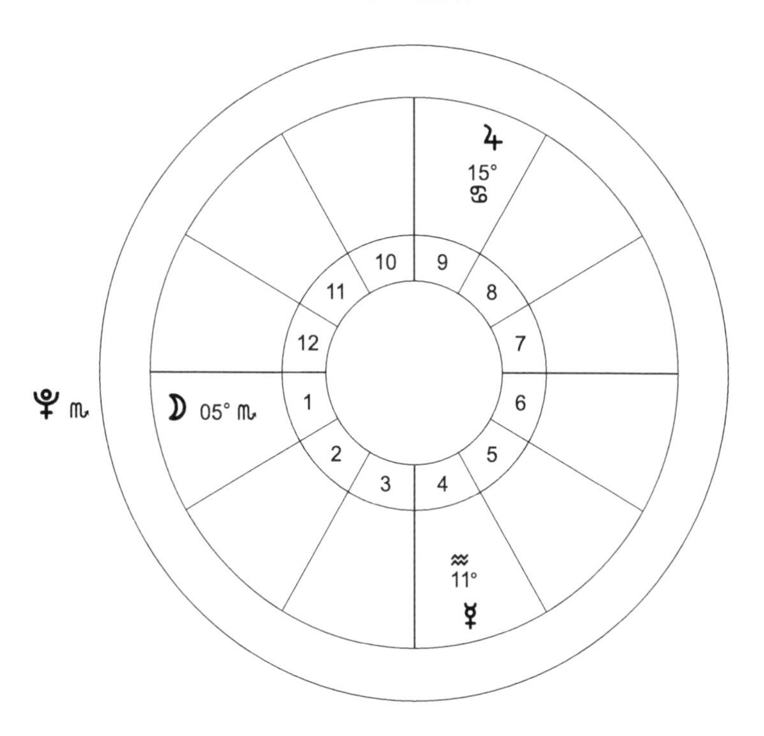

Laura was a young housewife and mother. She could not remember much of her childhood and she did not know why. As Pluto squared her Mercury and conjoined her Moon, she began to have horrible flashbacks to a time long ago. She thought she remembered being raped at a very young age by a family friend. She went into therapy to help her cope with the memories and to also bring them to the surface. Gradually the interval between 3 and 12 years of age began to fill in and it was not a happy time.

Laura spent many days crying alone after the children went to school. She smashed empty glass bottles on the basement walls trying to release her rage. Image after image rose and haunted her. It was particularly upsetting that her parents were still best friends with her attacker. She could not face another holiday with this person around. After harboring the secret for many months, she finally began to tell others. Not everyone believed her and this was hard on Laura emotionally.

She stuck to her story and one day sent a certified letter to her rapist, telling him of her memories and accusing him of the attacks. He denied the accusations, but Laura did not back down. Next, she decided to visit her parents and personally tell them of the trauma. She and her therapist rehearsed the meeting many times, and ultimately, Laura was able to tell her parents about the various incidents. She was not sure they would believe her, but she had to have some semblance of power after such a long time of powerlessness. She knew the truth even if they could not accept it. As it turned out, they supported her one hundred percent and shun their longtime friend. It was very important that they believe her. This calmed Laura's nerves. She knew her children and the other grandchildren would be protected from this man.

Pluto transits to Venus

Pluto transits to Venus indicate intense emotional involvements. New relationships begun at this time are especially compelling and kinetic for reasons you do not quite understand. Unconscious forces play a major role in these attractions. Like a moth to a flame, you are drawn to a particular individual without understanding why. In the beginning, the perceived loss of control and diminished rationality is disconcerting. Enthusiasm is high and you might feel obsessed. Regardless of what you think or plan, you end up reacting to situations in a spontaneous and revealing manner. Your usual psychological defenses don't seem to work while all your unconscious complexes are laid bare for the world to see. A persistent sense of vulnerability becomes coupled with your growing need for intimacy. If you are able to keep your defenses lowered, a relationship begun at this time can be most rewarding.

Potential or existing partners might exhibit a new and troubling flaw which may or may not be serious. In all relationships, considerable emotional growth can occur if you work with faults, and become aware of the unconscious urges and psychological games played by both parties. These ploys are barriers to further intimacy and must be recognized. Learning to deal effectively with these influences affects the success of the relationship. It is a good time for counseling of any kind, especially marriage or relationship counseling.

Situational barriers include attraction to married, gay, or bisexual partners, those living in a different locality, or those who cannot be fully present or involved for one reason or another. These preexisting impediments to intimacy were probably known or suspected before the relationship began.

Psychological impediments to intimacy are those unconscious complexes which distort reality and destroy trust. These include, but are not limited to, possessiveness, obsessive thinking, sexual fantasies, compulsive behaviors, and controlling attitudes.

Power is an issue in both intimate and casual relationships. Individuals who learn to trust, compromise, and share power see their relationships deepen and transform. Accommodating the emotional needs of others breeds increased understanding as long as you do not compromise self and surrender too much power.

Those who are unable to reach compromises should let go of passé relationships before they become locked in power struggles. Combatants view their fates as dependent on the whims of others. They feel powerless to control their own destiny until they have resolved some issue to their personal satisfaction. They resort to controlling behaviors as the only solution. Within this kind of power struggle, manipulative techniques are the main weapons; sex and money become the main issues.

Financially, Pluto transits to Venus indicate strong financial changes or complex monetary arrangements. Salary changes are common and may result from a career move, relocation, leave of absence without pay, cutback in hours, or retirement. On the other hand, ambition can cause your salary to rise dramatically, especially if your earnings are based on commissions or profit-sharing. Those who are self-employed experience monetary ups and downs. If your financial status depends on another's resources, a struggle over shared money is likely.

The goal here is to experience personal power in relationships and power over your own financial situation. By gaining insight into your behavior and the behavior of others, you can master both areas of concern. (See the example chart for Pluto transiting Mars.)

Pluto transits to Mars

When Pluto transits Mars, actions are not truly conscious or planned out. There is an acute awareness of the interplay between what appears to be directed activities and unconscious motivations. One does not just set career goals; one is driven to succeed. Compulsions and obsessions, healthy or not, are common since many psychological issues and complexes are indigenous to the scenarios you are involved in. With very negative situations, fears arise and phobias develop. The psychological influences affecting you spring unsolicited from your own unconscious, but are more likely to arise from your encounters with another. Generally, you must deal with this person regularly, and he or she may or may not be totally rational. Reacting from the gut level can become the standard mode of operation for those who do not work toward a greater understanding of these forces.

Control issues are likely during this time, and some individuals get locked into power struggles. In this type of situation, you are both able to manipulate others and subject to manipulation yourself. Surreptitious actions or underhanded maneuvers are also possible. Rather than battling with someone else, you can instead, (or also), be locked into a power struggle with yourself. One man with Pluto transiting his Mars was seriously wounded by a past relationship. He recognized the need to deal with unconscious anger and develop a philosophy for handling future anger-producing situations. During this transit, he met and was compulsively drawn to a new relationship. The loss of control over the inhibitions to intimacy frightened him. Consequently, the scene was set, and the interplay between the unconscious obsession to resolve the anger issues, and fear of being hurt again dominated the involvement.

Efforts to consciously control yourself will be thwarted until you gain insight into the problem at hand. The man was both irresistibly drawn, and yet frightened by the attraction until he began to resolve issues from the original relationship. This cleared the way for a more meaningful interchange.

Understanding psychological forces and learning to work with them rather than against can lead to productive encounters. Use insight to break bad habits and negative attitudes. The ability to comprehend new knowledge fostered by the unconscious leads to new power over your own actions and the situations you are involved in. It is at this point that realistic control over behavior begins.

Heather was married to a verbally abusive man for many years. She eventually left him and started a new life on her own in a distant state, but she never divorced her husband or sought a formal separation agreement. He still carried her on his health insurance policy and gave her a little money from time to time. Heather worked to support herself, but she always struggled with limited funds. During the years they were separated, her husband grew fairly wealthy unbeknownst to her. There was little contact between the two parties until Heather's husband decided to remarry and asked for a formal divorce.

It was during the divorce proceedings that Heather learned how much her husband was worth and that she had been a fool not to get a separation agreement before she left. Many years had passed and

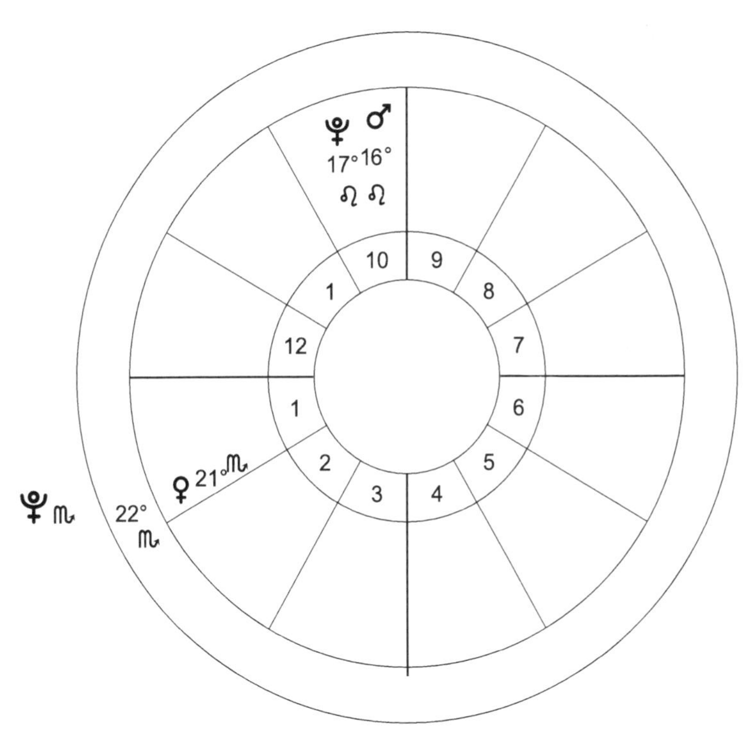

it was impossible to recover funds. The court's position was that since she left without anything, she was not entitled to much now. Her husband cut off all extra money. While Heather continued to struggle to feed and clothe herself, her husband's new love arrived at the court house decked out in jewels and fancy clothes.

The stress eventually wore on Heather's health and she became seriously ill. When she submitted her medical bills to the insurance company, her husband received and cashed the health insurance refund checks, leaving her seriously in debt. Heather's anger grew and so did her chronic illness which became more and more debilitating. Eventually she could no longer work. She thought that the judge would recognize her disability and award her a fair amount of money plus permanent maintenance. He did not. Heather found it difficult to go to court and speak in her own defense though her husband told lies about their relationship. This hurt her case. In the end, Heather was given a small sum of money from the house they owned jointly valued at the time of the separation. That's it.

Externally, Heather was not in a position of power at the beginning of the divorce proceedings. She had not anticipated the next step when she left her husband years ago. The choices she made proved disastrous. She was not internally powerful either. She vacillated between feeling like a victim of her husband's continuing abuse and feeling guilty about asking for money. She was as angry with herself as she was at her husband. The internal conflict wore on her body until eventually she was ill. She never took a definitive position and worked against herself in all matters. This left the door open for someone else to assume power.

Conclusion

As you read through the stories presented here in this article, you cannot help but notice how dissimilar the people and situations are, and what diverse choices they all made. Some took the bull by the horns, while others choose a gentle route. Some tried to catch up from years of stagnation, others were ahead of their time. Sensitivity to Uranian impulses, subtle Neptunian awareness, or Plutonian urges for power influenced the type of situation faced (internal or external) and the strength of the response (active or passive). Some choices were better than others, but there are rarely any clear-cut wrong decisions. The complexity of a Uranus, Neptune, or Pluto transit implies dilemma. It may be impossible to be right or wrong. But it is important that you learn. This you will do, willingly or not.

One cannot take these outer planets lightly. Taken individually they represent tremendous growth potential. But taken as a group, as they presently are, the possibility for accelerated evolution exists. Now more than ever, we have ways to go beyond, if only we would choose.

APPENDIX

Uranus, Neptune, and Pluto

URANUS

Key concepts: flowing movement, freedom, and change

During a Uranus transit you learn:

1. about ease and flow in the river of life versus difficulty, hardship, and being stuck
2. what frees you up to move in a natural way that is correct for you
3. what binds you, is limiting, or forces you to be unnatural in your movement
4. what leads to creativity, inspiration, insight, freedom, change, and originality

Possible Events:

1. unexpected occurrences and surprises
2. disruption of plans, major changes, fluctuations, planned or unexpected
3. breakdowns, repairs, and needed adjustments
4. accidents
5. decisions and changes you avoid that are then made for you by others or circumstances
6. upheaval
7. separations

Psychological Influences:

1. restlessness, erratic impulses, rebelliousness
2. unpredictable breaks in routines
3. desire for freedom
4. need for change, modernization, or upgrade
5. tendency to take a risk

Making Choices with the Outer Planets Transits

Positive Uranian Strategies:

1. ask questions
2. observe
3. reassess
4. consider alternatives
5. prepare
6. choose
7. then change

Negative Uranian Responses:

1. fear of change, fear of becoming stuck, approach-avoidance anxiety, ambivalence
2. controlling, resisting, and clinging, codependency
3. chaos, crisis management, becoming undependable, erratic, or reactionary
4. struggling to fit a square peg is a round hole

Spiritual Attainments:

1. internally or externally detachment, freeing yourself
2. insightful intelligence, inspiration
3. creativity
4. fluidity, like water flowing down hill, becoming unstoppable
5. improvements and change, modernizations
6. raising the energy level, spiritual upgrade

NEPTUNE

Key concepts: sensitivity leading to insight, unconditional love, trust, compassion, and awakening

During a Neptune transit:

1. you learn through an increase in emotional, intuitive, and spiritual sensitivity
2. you experience positive oneness and negative oneness with life and others
3. information and your point of reference blurs, there can be disorientation through a loss of definition
4. logical and learned knowledge can be eclipsed by intuition and higher understanding
5. cause and effect thinking can be superseded by coincidental awareness
6. you gain insight through prayer, meditation, communing with nature, creativity, and art
7. you learn to trust yourself and your gut

Possible Events:

1. deception, denial, distortion, disillusionment, despair, hopelessness
2. confusion, uncertainty, disorganization
3. fanaticism, strange beliefs, misguided actions
4. food, pet, and environmental allergies, or unexplained/difficult to diagnose maladies
5. what you are told is different from what you intuit, what you believe is different from your experience
6. isolation, self-sacrifice, victimization

Making Choices with the Outer Planets Transits

Psychological Influences:

1. increased emotional and intuitive sensitivity and awareness
2. call to understand and work with subtle and not so subtle human and spiritual energies
3. asked to give more, love better, and comprehend more than in the past
4. trust, step into the unknown without guarantees by putting one foot in front of the other
5. given choices, deciding what is real and true

Positive Neptune Strategies:

1. trust your gut, yourself, and higher sources to discern the truth
2. listen in the silence, pray, meditate, walk in nature
3. stay true to your real self, higher self, and your principles
4. proceed in an ethical manner

Negative Neptune Responses:

1. fighting to know definitively, seeking truth from others, focusing on details, logic, rules
2. believing in and trusting others more than yourself, hence becoming misled
3. self-sacrifice to the point of being drained, becoming vulnerable, emphasizing doing rather than being
4. confusion, disorganization, deception, fraud, lack of cohesiveness, wandering
5. fear, anxiety, worry
6. escapism through drugs, alcohol, withdrawal, blocking or ignoring influences
7. allergies, asthma, hypochondria, sensory overload
8. judgments, condemnations, sense of betrayal

Uranus, Neptune, and Pluto

Spiritual Attainments:

1. ability to abide in the mystery, trust the irrational, timeless principles, and deeper meaning
2. true compassion, unconditional love, acceptance, higher understanding, empathy
3. true service to others and self, walking the talk, oneness, as above, so below consistency and alignment, sense of purpose
4. spiritual/religious awakening, awareness of and adherence to the spirit of the law
5. emphasis on being rather than doing
6. creativity, inspiration

Making Choices with the Outer Planets Transits

PLUTO

Key concepts: empowerment, transformation, release, letting go, psychological insight

During a Pluto transit:

1. you learn the balance of power is changing in your life, you can gain or lose power, or become empowered
2. you learn the source and extent of personal power/ambition along with boundaries/obstacles
3. you must decide how to best use power while remaining true to yourself, your ethics, and priorities
4. you must be clear about what you want within those parameters
5. you learn to discern the most powerful and appropriate response and course of action
6. you remember and past history comes due

Possible Events:

1. power struggle over money, sex, morality, and anything else important to someone
2. major renovations or changes in regard to house, family, lifestyle, career, and relationships
3. death or illness
4. complications, complex situations without good clear-cut answers or choices
5. loss of control, matters are out of your hands, there is nothing you can do to change the situation, need for acceptance

Psychological influences:

1. ambition, desire to take on position and responsibility, control, wanting to advance and gain power

2. emotional review of the past and the unconscious, which can be overwhelming, inner turmoil
3. letting go of what is old and passé
4. release
5. acute awareness, know more than you want to know

Positive Plutonian Strategies:

1. let go of what is not important while remaining true to self, let go of what people think of you
2. apply knowledge and understanding by taking action and getting results
3. de-escalate situations by anticipating problems, craziness, overreactions, enter therapy
4. foster win-win situations, empower yourself and others, becoming nonthreatening, and calming
5. renovate, renew, clean house, streamline, grow
6. know when to let go, detach, denature your psychological buttons

Negative Plutonian responses:

1. power struggles, control issues, rubber-band booby-traps, manipulation
2. escalation, reactionary responses, emotional overload, fear and anger becomes louder than insight or reason
3. surrender, loss of power, power leakage, vacillation leading to further complications
4. black and white polarized situations, blame game, hung up on proving the opponent wrong
5. frozen, stuck, artificially sustaining passé situations
6. mentally unbalanced, unconscious debris magnifies and distorts, overreactions, and threatening behavior
7. stooping to conquer, physical or verbal battles, fixation of weaponry

Making Choices with the Outer Planets Transits

Spiritual Attainments:

1. transformation
2. transmutation
3. transcendence
4. empowerment of self and others

Made in the USA
Columbia, SC
30 October 2022